THINGS I WANT TO SAY AT WORK BUT CAN'T

Cuss Word Coloring Book For Adults
Featuring 35 Swear pages To Color
For Stress Relief And Relaxation

Need More Cuss Word Adults Coloring Book

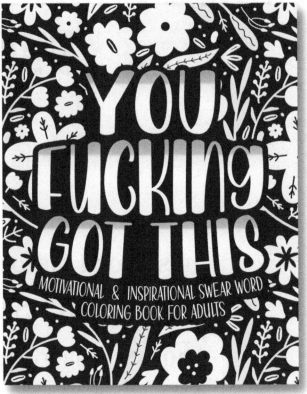

Swear Word Coloring Book

ISBN:B0B4HYGZ1L

You Fucking Got This

ISBN:B0B3RL7DCS

Claim Your Freeßie

Follow us on Instagram:

@bokaplaysyripe

Share Your Artwork:
#bokaplaysyripe

Find us on Facebook:

Bokaplaysyripe - Coloring Books

ISBN: 9798834502951

CHECK OUT OUR OTHER BOOKS:

www.bokaplaysyripe.com

For questions and customer service, email us at
bokaplay.syripe@yahoo.com

Color Test Page

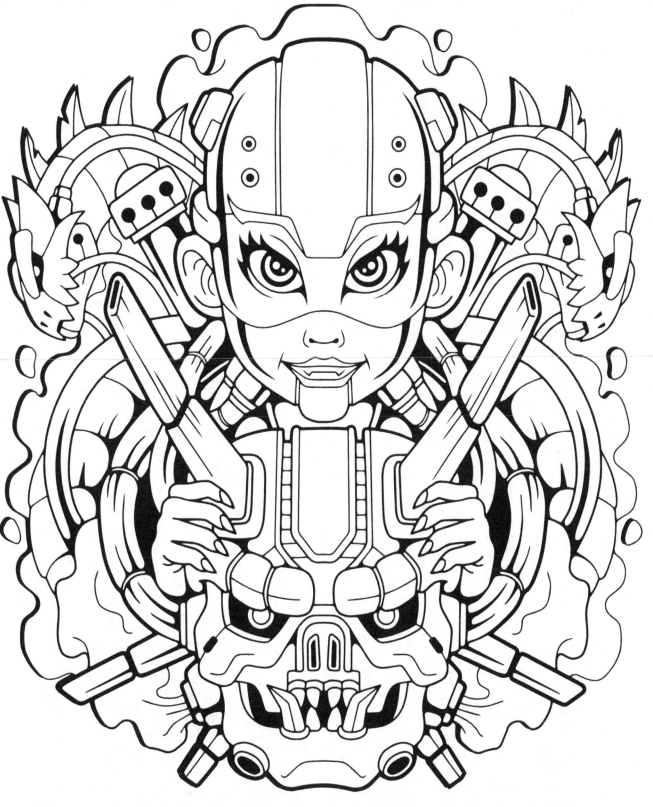

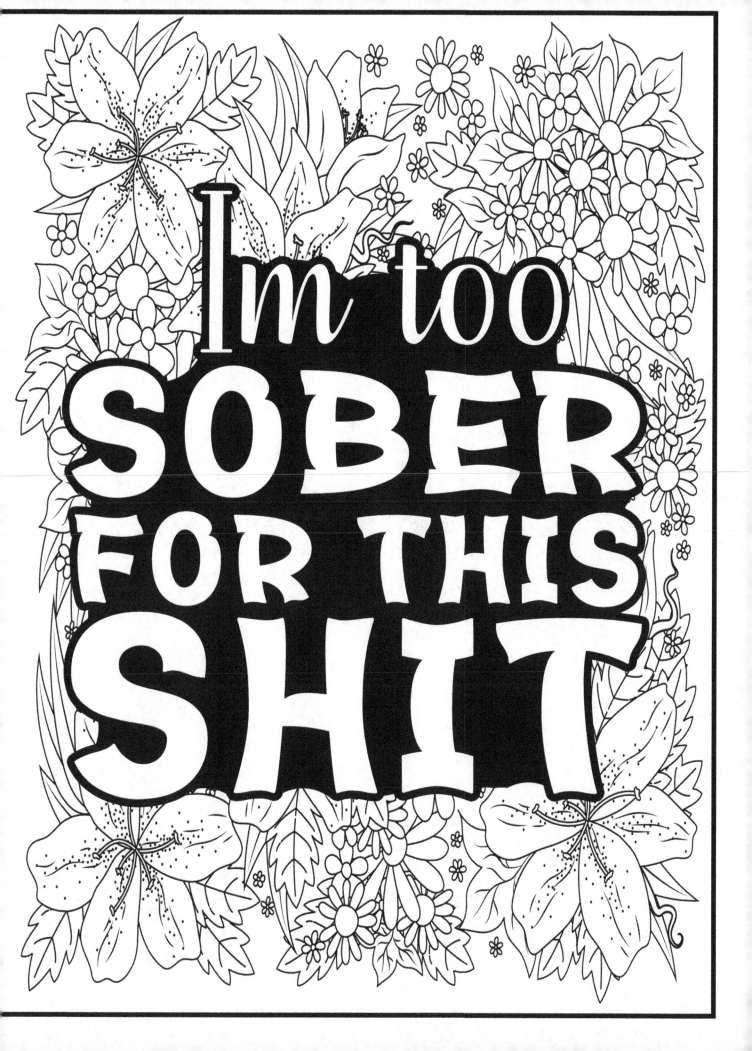

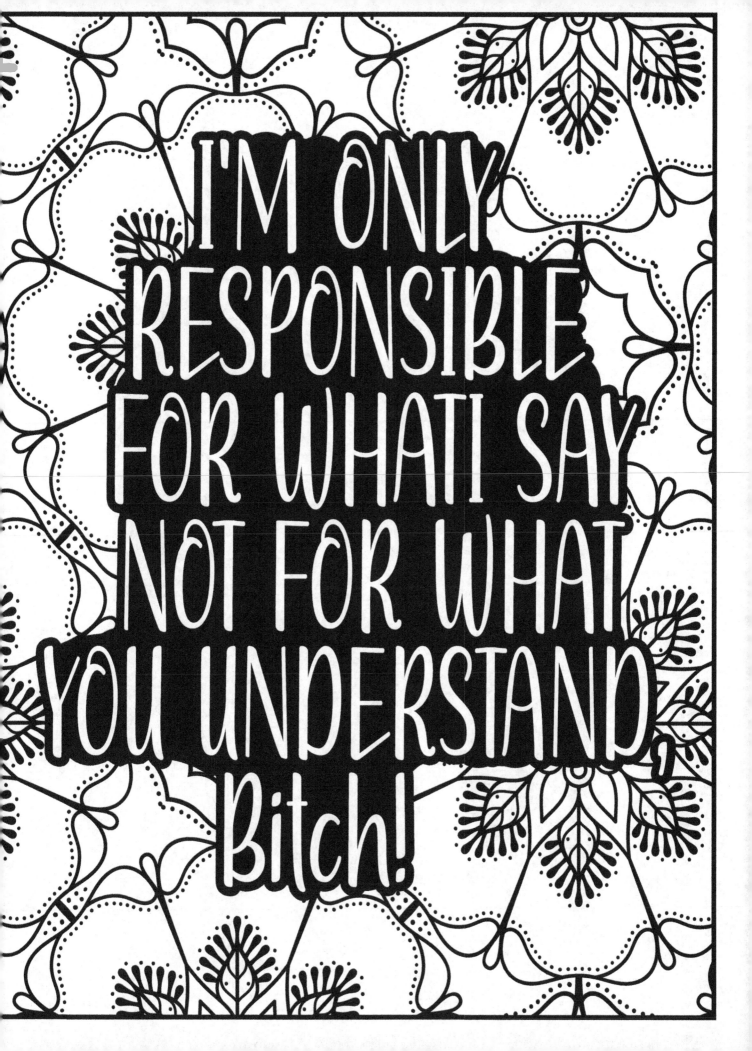

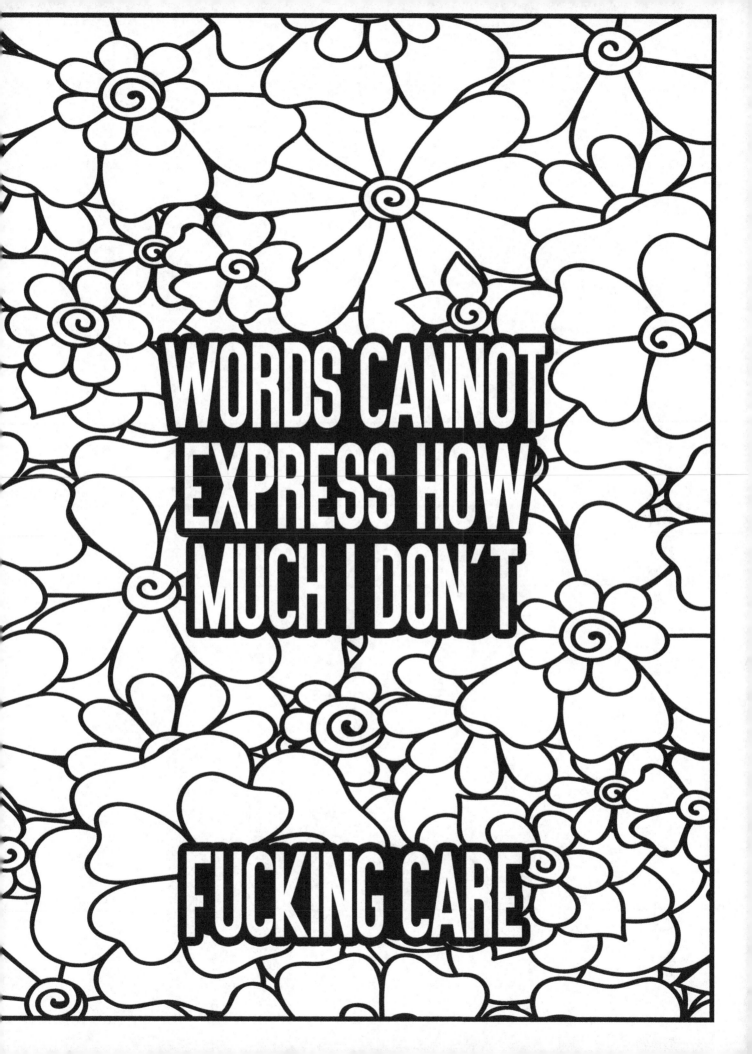

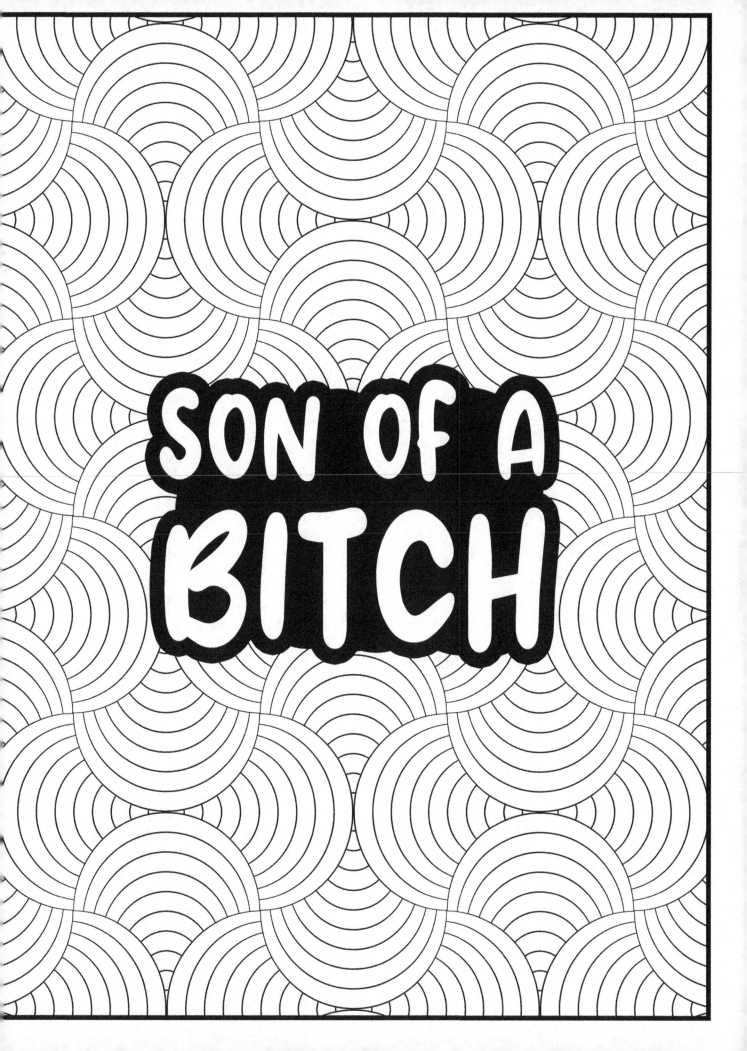

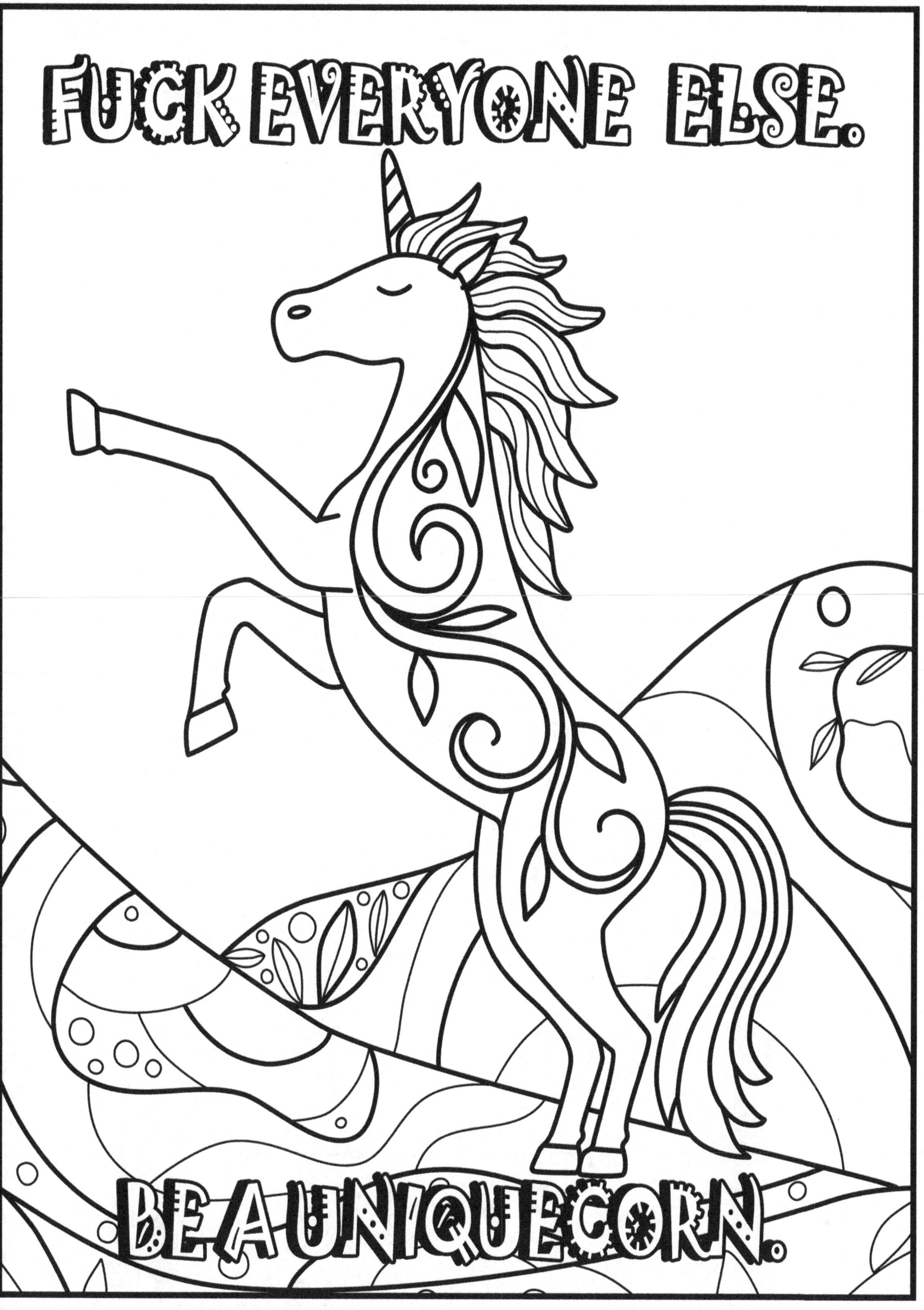
FUCK EVERYONE ELSE.
BE A UNIQUECORN.

DON'T BE A DICK

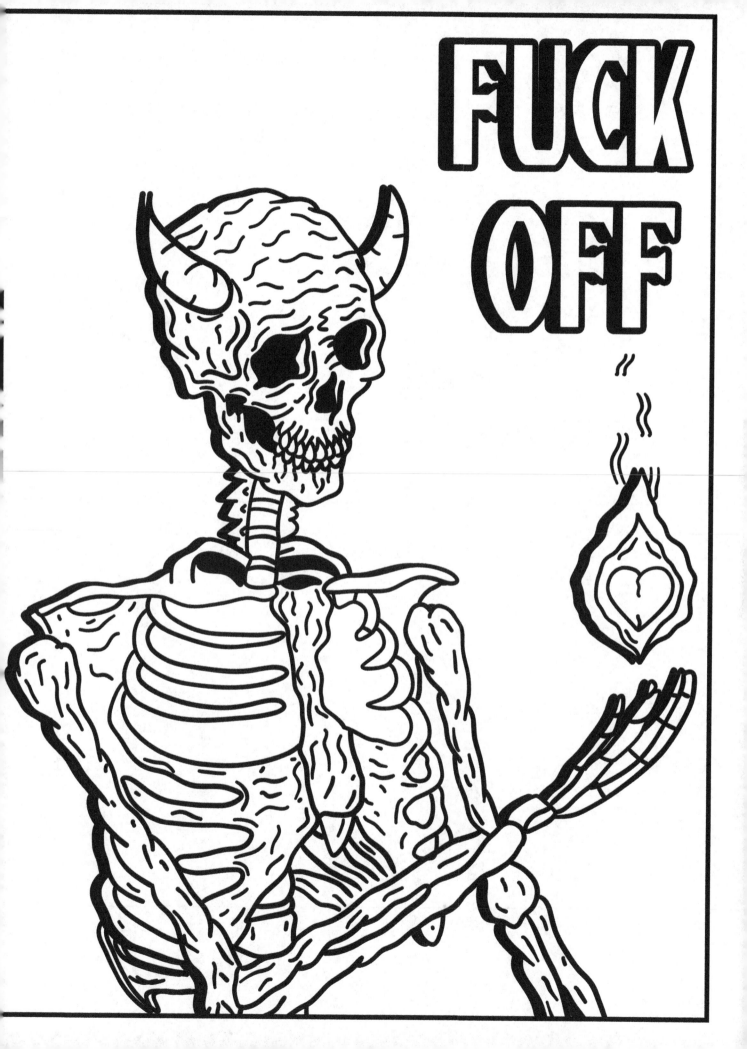

ASSHOLE

fuck pandemic

Made in United States
North Haven, CT
21 December 2022

29983033R00043